SIGHT SINGING MADE EZ!

BOOK FOUR - Advanced SSA Treble Voices

Music by RONNIE SANDERS

A Complete 18-week Music Reading Curriculum Designed for
Middle and **High School** Advanced Girl's choirs

For more assistance in sight singing, please find:
www.ronniesanders.net

Publications by Ronnie Sanders:

Sight Singing Made EZ! Book One
Beginning Voices - Unison
BCM1402

Sight Singing Made EZ! Book Two
Intermediate 2-Part SA Treble Voices
BCM1501

Sight Singing Made EZ! Book Three
Intermediate 2-Part TB Men's Voices
BCM1503

Sight Singing Made EZ! Book Four
Advanced SSA Treble Voices
BCM1506

Sight Singing Made EZ! Book Five
Advanced TTB Men's Voices
BCM1507

Sight Singing Made EZ! Book Six
Advanced SAB Mixed Voices
BCM1601

Sight Singing Made EZ! Book Seven
Intermediate SAB Mixed Voices
BCM1603

This page was intentionally left blank – not sure why – I just felt like it.

Sight Singing Made EZ!
BOOK FOUR - Advanced Three-Part Treble Voices

Imagine yourself as a high school pole vaulting coach. Let's say your star athlete has just jumped over the bar set at 14 feet. Would you, as their coach, continue to set the bar at 14 feet? You'd likely raise the bar a little higher to challenge your start athlete, right? That's why I wrote *Sight Singing Made EZ*.

These musical exercises will challenge your singers, and occasionally your conducting skills, as students learn to master the art of singing at sight together.

Many sight-singing instruction books focus mainly on the notes and rhythms. This book offers a more comprehensive musical approach to choral sight singing. Students will get the chance to sing the correct notes and rhythms, and also see that musicianship can be enhanced by reading the dynamics and articulations *at first sight.*

Each week's lesson gives the choir teacher a simple-to-use vocal exercise for augmenting classroom music reading instruction. There is an eight-measure exercise for every day of an 18-week semester. Each week concentrates on a specific key. There are four weeks of material in the keys of F, G and Eb. There are also exercises in the keys of C, Bb, A and D.

Sight Singing Made EZ will be a wonderful addition to your daily routine. Teachers - it's all planned out for you. By the end of the 18 weeks, students will know what it takes to read the ENTIRE SCORE - not just the notes and rhythms!

Ronnie Sanders
Website: www.ronniesanders.net
e-mail: info@ronniesanders.net

SIGHT SINGING MADE EZ!

SSA Advanced Treble

Music by RONNIE SANDERS

Week 1

Sight Singing Made EZ - Advanced Treble

WWW.RONNIESANDERS.NET

Week 2

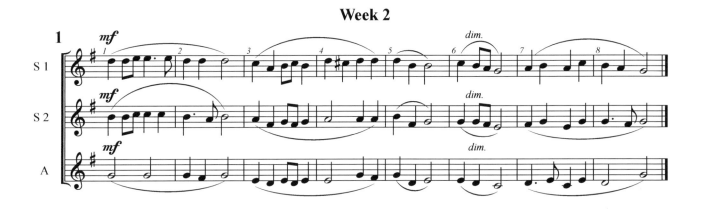

BCM1506

Helpful Hint Number 1

Just so you'll know, I write these exercises for my advanced girls' choir and use them every day. I often figure out creative ways to mix up the exercises so that the girls will read 16 measures of music every day - not just the 8 measures printed.

For example, I often have choir read their own line, then, I have them switch parts, the altos, for example will read the soprano II part, and the soprano I's may read the alto part and the soprano II's will read the soprano I part.

The next day I may mix it up completely. I might ask all the girls in the front row to read the soprano I line, the second row of girls read the soprano II line and the back row of girls to read the alto line. It keeps rehearsals interesting and the students never know which part they're going to sing.

Ronnie Sanders
Website: www.ronniesanders.net
e-mail: info@ronniesanders.net

List ways to switch arrangement of singers:

Week 3

Sight Singing Made EZ - Advanced Treble

Week 4

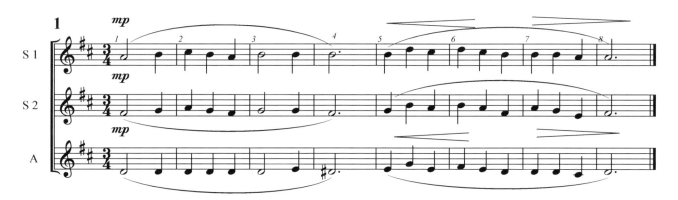

BCM1506

Sight Singing Made EZ - Advanced Treble

WWW.RONNIESANDERS.NET

Sight Singing Made EZ!
BOOK FOUR - Advanced Three-Part Treble Voices

Helpful Hint Number 2

As you may have noticed by now, I have included at least one altered syllable in every exercise. Good voice leading involves carefully approaching and resolving all altered pitches in a stepwise manner. Further, I will never write an unusual or awkward leap designed to "trick" a singer.

As I wrote these exercises, I kept a voice part from singing the diatonic pitch too quickly after it had been altered (I avoid singers encountering a *fa* for example, immediately after singing a *fi).*

For example, please find Exercise 4 in Week 5. Find the soprano altered C# in measure 26. Notice that the soprano I does NOT sing the C natural again until measure 30 - four measures *after* the C#. This kind of placement allows the singer's ear to readjust the intonation back to the diatonic scale.

As you listen the students sing the altered pitches, make sure they are perfectly in tune.

Ronnie Sanders
Website: www.ronniesanders.net
e-mail: info@ronniesanders.net

Notes on exercises - anticipated problems in tuning:

Sight Singing Made EZ - Advanced Treble

WWW.RONNIESANDERS.NET

Week 5

Sight Singing Made EZ - Advanced Treble

WWW.RONNIESANDERS.NET

Week 6

Sight Singing Made EZ - Advanced Treble

4

5

Week 7

1

2

Sight Singing Made EZ - Advanced Treble

Week 8

Sight Singing Made EZ - Advanced Treble

WWW.RONNIESANDERS.NET

Sight Singing Made EZ!
BOOK FOUR - Advanced Three-Part Treble Voices

Helpful Hint Number 3

Just a word about some of the choices I made about fermatas (fermati?). Please find Exercise 2 in Week 10. Notice the fermata in measure 15. Any conductor can conduct a 4/4 pattern - easy, right? But to cue *just the altos* after the fermata *then cue the sopranos* in measure 16 requires a quick hand - and clear gestures.

As you and the singers hold the fermata, give the choir a sharp cut-off from the held note. The cutoff can be your preparation cue for the alto entrance after the fermata. Breathe with the altos as you give them a cue with a sharp ictus for their entrance.

As the altos sing their eighth note, gesture to the sopranos to come in with the right hand - all while gently giving a decrescendo motion with your left hand for the rest of Measure 16. Easy, right? (Of course, right?)

Remember, the same gesture you use for the cutoff from the fermata may be used as a preparation cue for the next entrance whether or not the next entrance is an eighth note or quarter note (find Week 11, Exercise 2, Measure 14).

Ronnie Sanders
Website: www.ronniesanders.net
e-mail: info@ronniesanders.net

Notes on gestures for exercises:

Sight Singing Made EZ - Advanced Treble

WWW.RONNIESANDERS.NET

Week 9

BCM1506

Sight Singing Made EZ - Advanced Treble

WWW.RONNIESANDERS.NET

5

Week 10

1

2

3

Sight Singing Made EZ - Advanced Treble

WWW.RONNIESANDERS.NET

Week 11

Week 12

Sight Singing Made EZ - Advanced Treble

BCM1506

Sight Singing Made EZ - Advanced Treble

WWW.RONNIESANDERS.NET

Week 13

Sight Singing Made EZ - Advanced Treble

WWW.RONNIESANDERS.NET

Week 14

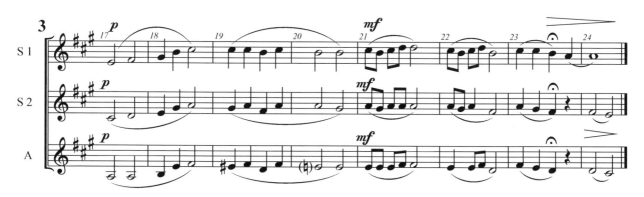

BCM1506

Sight Singing Made EZ - Advanced Treble

Week 15

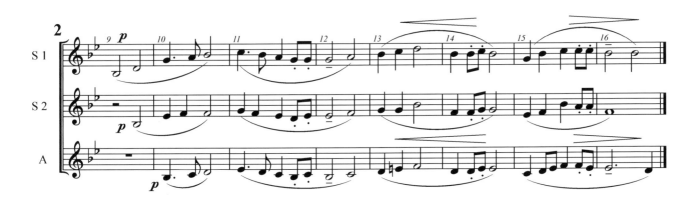

Week 16

Sight Singing Made EZ - Advanced Treble

WWW.RONNIESANDERS.NET

Week 17

BCM1506

Sight Singing Made EZ - Advanced Treble

Week 18

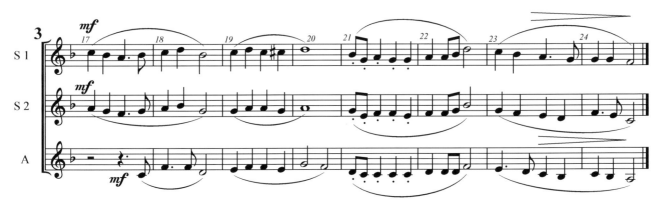

Sight Singing Made EZ - Advanced Treble

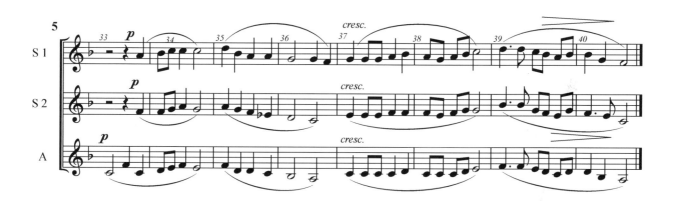

Made in the USA
San Bernardino, CA
04 January 2019